LIFE'S A BITCH

: A brief guide on dealing with it

By Geraint Rhys Benney Life and Spiritual Coach

Life's a Bitch
A brief guide on dealing with it
Written by Geraint Rhys Benney
life and spiritual coach.

Chapters

Introduction

Hello and welcome to Life's a Bitch, my name is Geraint Rhys Benney - a Dr, psychologist, professor, mystic, saviour, guru I am not, and I do not proclaim to be. I'm a man, a normal one, flaws and all. What I am though, is a believer, a believer in the power of self-belief, a believer in following our dreams and creating a life lived on our terms. Over the last few years I have been on a journey of discovery; I wanted to know what the meaning of life was, if there even is a meaning at all. What I found out pretty quickly was that yes, there is a meaning to life and that meaning is living it. Why else are we here, if not to experience life itself and to live it to its full extent and potential? The difficult part of living life is the how part: how do we live it to its full potential? How do we live it happily? I'm writing this guide because I believe I have found a way to make the most of what we have in front of us, and to take the next step in living a life that's on our terms. It's not a quick fix or a miracle cure for what life throws at us, its more of a method of living, a way of life, even. It's not religious, it's not a fad, it's not brain washing or a new-wave thinking cult - it is what it is and it's you who's in charge. You believe what you want to believe, you have that choice, that's the point. Once we become at peace with ourselves and accept that life is a bitch, we can start living. I don't believe that we need to believe in a greater being to become great; I believe that we are great beings - great ourselves - and that with self-belief we can achieve unbelievable things. Before you read on (and I hope you will), I'd like you to approach what I talk about with an open mind, take in what I'm saying and think about it logically, give it - and yourself - the opportunity to create wonderful things when working together. I don't claim to know all the answers, but what I do know is that happiness begins within, and once we find it within, life begins to make more sense in a world of confusion. Anyway, I hope you enjoy Life's a Bitch and that it gives you a belief in yourself like it has given me a belief in myself.

Geraint Rhys Benney

CHAPTER 1

Life's a Bitch

Life is a bitch, it really is; no matter what we try and do, we always seem to end up back where we started - or even worse, somewhere we don't want to be. We live good lives, we try to be the best person we can by always putting others first and doing the right thing; but we lose touch with ourselves in the process. It's like living on a rollercoaster and it's out of control. If we were all truly honest with ourselves, how many of us would admit to feeling that we sometimes have no control of where we are going or what we are doing? I know I have, and often still do, but there is an alternative way of doing things, a different way of looking at life and making it work for us on our terms. Why, or how it works, I don't know and don't care; it works, that's all that matters to me and that's all that should matter to you, its just a matter of excepting a different way of living and reality. We don't know how most things in the world work, we just accept that they do and get on with life; this is no different. We have to be in it to win it.

So who am I to give advice? That's a good question. Who am I to give advice on how to live your life? I'm you and you are me: we are the same but different in many ways, we all have our story. Mine is that I have suffered great loss, had plenty of ups and downs throughout my life, and an on going relationship with depression since childhood. The story of my past life was ruling my present and future life and how I felt on a daily basis: my life story was running its own narrative without any control from myself. It felt like I was drifting on an ocean with no idea which direction to go and without a paddle to get me there anyway. I had to start again, I had to become me again, I had to take back control of my story and start living it on my terms. The first step I took on my journey was consulting with my doctor. I have a very forward and understanding doctor and we both decided that taking medication was not the answer to my problems as it would only mask my issues rather than solve them. I tried counselling and found it very helpful, but I know sitting down talking about our feelings to a stranger is a terrifying prospect for some - and that's mostly down to self-confidence - but for me it helped. It didn't solve my problem but it gave me courage to ask myself the questions I needed answered. Yes, it took me some time to be able to say how I felt, to admit my own failings, and to bring all of my issues out in the open to deal with head on instead of hiding away. I had buried my head in the sand for a long time and it was time to start holding it high for once for all to see. I read every self-help book I could get my hands on, trying to find the key to happiness, trying to find what I was missing, what was preventing my life from feeling complete, how I could fill the void.

I don't think I need to rabbit on about what my problems are; they are irrelevant in the bigger picture of things. That's one of the things I have learned about my life and life in general: our problems are entirely irrelevant to our happiness. For as far back as I can remember, I had taken myself and life far too seriously; whenever something went wrong I took it to heart, I took it personally, but really it wasn't personal at all, it was just life being a bitch, and life is a bitch to everyone. It was my reactions to life that posed the problems, not life itself. To some extent I was creating my own misfortune. We are taught from a young age to be afraid of the unknown, to have fear of failing and to not make fools of ourselves; whether it's from teachers, peers, or family. We are setting ourselves up to fail without even realising - it's been bred into us. But 'fear not' as they say, because it's not irreversible. We can make changes and it's not as hard as some make it out to be, but we have got to want to change for it to happen. We have all met people in our lives that say they want to change but are not really willing to make any effort to do so: it's easier to be a victim than to take any kind of action or make any effort and why not? It's easier to blame others for our misfortunes and bad luck, that way we don't have to take any responsibility, we can just complain and pity ourselves. But you know as well as I do that gets us nowhere, other than where we have already been, and as we have found out, that's not where we belong, we can achieve more. I'm no expert, especially not on 'life', and I don't claim to be. I am a student of life and I'm not an expert of all the things I talk about, I still have a lot to learn - I believe we all do - and I have found all of the following methods incredibly useful in improving my life. My theory is: if it's helped me, then maybe it can help other people, and by you reading at least this far tells me that other person could be you.

So, "how do we turn our lives around?" I hear you ask. Well, in a number of ways, but I'm going to be totally honest with you: there is no easy way to change; it takes a lot of effort. Nothing comes easily, however, it is achievable and accessible with a little self-belief and courage. Anything is possible.

CHAPTER 2

Self-Belief

Before we start anything new, we have to believe we can achieve our chosen goals; there is no point even starting if we don't believe we can reach the finish line. Hands up how many of us worry what others think about our actions, how many of us relish the reassurance of our family, friends and even complete strangers? I know I did. I'm not saying that we shouldn't consider other peoples' feelings or opinions - far from it, of course we should. What I'm saying is, we only need to be concerned with how we feel about our life, as it is our life, our problem, and most importantly, it needs our solutions. Whilst worrying about everyone else's opinions, we are putting our lives in their hands, we are letting them control our happiness, and we depend on them to tell us how to feel. This needs to stop as soon as possible.

Society has a general misconception that happiness is found in external objects; material possessions, other people, events even, but happiness comes from deep inside of us and only we can create happiness, happiness can't create us. Each morning I tell myself I'm going to have an amazing day, and I say these words with such conviction that they become feelings. I feel the words I speak, they penetrate the deepest core of my soul, and I believe them, every single word. It's a simple but effective affirmation and I use it daily - without fail - and I can promise you it works, if you practice with belief your days will become anything you want them to.

I was told once that wanting to love myself was egotistical, but I can assure you it's not. Loving ourselves is not egotistical, loving ourselves is magical; how do we expect anyone else to fall in love with us if we can't do it ourselves? There is nothing less attractive than self-pity, and that covers all aspects of life. The only people that we are going to attract are people in the same boat: if we are negative we find people on the same negative vibration, and we will almost inevitably end up wallowing in each other's negativity, making life even more draining and difficult. Please don't take my words lightly; low self-esteem and depression are subjects I take very seriously. They can make life unbearable and crushing, and I sympathize with anyone who suffers this mind-set, but if I can help ease the struggle and give hope to just one person, then writing this will have been more than worth it.

Ok, "how do we start loving who we are?" is a question that we can only answer individually. I can provide the tools to help sculpt, but you have to do the hard work and chisel out all of your insecurities. As I said, each morning I tell myself I'm going to have an amazing day; when I started doing this they were only words, but as I persisted, I really did mean what I said. Beginning my day with positivity, by repeating my affirmation and avoiding any kind of negativity - from everyday news broadcasts, newspapers and general gossip - my days improved drastically. I know what you're thinking, but please read on, it works on so many levels and you've come this far you can't give up now can you? After all, what have you got to lose by trying something that can improve YOU?

As the weeks went on, I started giving myself extra little tasks, almost like a game I suppose: the rule of this game was to make everyone a winner. I'd try and do something different each day to make it more interesting.

Let me give you some examples:

Monday - smile and make eye contact.
Tuesday – give compliments.
Wednesday - say 'thank you' and be grateful.
Thursday - only use positive words.
Friday - tell everyone you talk to that you hope they have an amazing weekend.
Saturday and Sunday - spend time with loved ones and friends.

I think you get my drift, but remember subtlety is key. Feeling happy and being positive are all states of mind, and by choosing to actively harness these feelings, we awaken a magical place deep inside of us - yes I know, I said magical. We all have day to day issues that can make us feel less than happy; the bus is late, we lose the house keys, we tip our drink, we literally get out of the wrong side of the bed and so on. Some days are a bitch, but it's how we react that counts. We can't change what's happened, and ranting or being angry and sore with a situation (and that's all these things are, situations), lets these factors determine our mood. Letting this happen means our life is never our own.

You were born, beating the odds by around 6 billion to 1. Yes, you; before you even took a breath you were a winner. You are special, extraordinary, a miracle in every way, and you have the ability to achieve incredible things. You ROCK. You read that correctly, I said you rock, and you can become whoever or whatever you choose to be.

As human beings, we are the dominant race on the planet, with great abilities and prospects - we made it to the moon and back despite being told it couldn't be done. It was all a result of self-belief, looking fear in the eye and making it happen. We have to be realistic with our goals without limiting ourselves, but even baby steps must have clear and definite goals. We have all had experiences that have made us so happy in that moment of time - no matter how big or small there are memories that can brighten our days when we think about them. I want you to close your eyes and imagine you're there now; imagine that feeling and carry it with you throughout the day today, consider it your first real task. I use this when I start feeling low; it helps me take back control of my emotions and puts me back on track.

As a second task, I want you to spend at least two weeks telling yourself - without fail - you are worthy of love, happiness and prosperity. You are worth every bead of sweat you shed. Tell yourself you are amazing, be the most positive person you can be. Talk about what you do want and not what you don't. The words we use on a daily basis are the building blocks for our lives, they are the foundation of our beliefs and actions: in plain English, we are not only what we think we are, we are what we talk and feel - so choose your words and feelings wisely. I don't want you to stop once the fortnight is over; in fact, I never want you to stop giving yourself praise. After a couple of weeks take some time and think about how many of the people around you have been impacted by your positivity? Your positivity can and will affect those around you without them even being aware. Try it out, it really works!

Nothing is set in stone, apart from stone itself, and even that can be broken down and reshaped. We can change if we want to, we can turn our frown into a smile, our unhappiness into happiness, our sorrow into joy - all we need is courage in ourselves. I remember being told on more than one occasion that I couldn't do something or that I wasn't the man for the job, to go and try something easier, something more compatible with my abilities. Well let me tell you now: if someone else is capable of doing it, then I can do it too. I'm made of the same things, all the same parts - apart from sexual organs in some instances, although in this day and age even that's possible! What I suppose I'm trying to say is: YES YOU CAN.

It may take time, it may take hard work, but if you can think it then give it a go. There is no failure. We don't fail, we learn, we adapt, and with perseverance, we can find a way to achieve.

CHAPTER 3

Fear

I can understand why people live their lives in fear. I've been there myself and it's not a nice place to live. It can consume every inch of us and it can literally possess us. Fear - just like Father Christmas - isn't real. It's a figment of our imaginations, and like Father Christmas, we choose to believe in it, ultimately giving it life. Please be assured that I'm not making light of anyone's fears; as I said – I am all too familiar, but I managed to find a way of living with it on my terms and hopefully you can too.

What is fear?

Fear is an unpleasant emotion or thought. It's the feeling we get when we are afraid or worried that something bad is going to happen. The feeling of fear has to be one of the greatest impediments to our progress. As humans, we will always feel fear, but we must be very careful not to empower it so that it influences our actions and decisions. It is the unfounded fear that is within us all that is undermining our confidence, determining who we are, and jeopardizing all our real hopes of success.

So how do we escape the clutches of fear?

We don't: we learn to live alongside it, we gave it life for a reason. You see, we need fear in our lives - it keeps us alive, it stops us walking off cliff edges, walking in front of buses, or getting married, even (there's that humour I'm grateful for). Fear can be a good thing if used correctly. Our relationship with fear stems from childhood - it's been drummed into us to fear the unknown.

Just like when we spoke about self-belief, we need to start to think about the positive, we need to think about the best outcome if we do the thing we fear, and not the worse.

If we fear something we want to do, then all we need do is ask ourselves a few simple questions:

Will I die?
Will I get physically hurt?
Will anyone die or get physically hurt?
Will I get arrested?

If the answer to the above questions are 'no', then go for gold. We're in safe hands. We are in the safest hands we could be in: we're in our own hands, the person who wants us to succeed the most. We don't fail in life, we learn, and if we can't do something then that's ok because we tried. We had a go, we made the effort, we may have grown as a person. It's all okay as long as we have improved ourselves, it's better to have tried and failed than to have never have tried at all, no regrets. There is a saying that goes, "the only thing to be fearful of, is fear itself", and I can assure you we don't need to fear our own capabilities. Is it the fear of failing or the fear of succeeding that really frightens us the most?

The only way of loosening the clutches of fear is looking it straight in the eyes and telling it that it should be scared of you. Stand in front of the mirror and shout at it! Tell it you are in charge! Rant, rave, jump up and down if it helps. Show it how ferocious you can be. Go on, do it. See how it makes you feel. It's not silly, it's invigorating, it's freeing, it's you taking charge and showing life who's boss. It's you believing in YOU. What other people think is irrelevant: they have their own fears, let them carry on with their insecurities. It's not as if you're asking them to change, and besides, only the weak try to belittle whilst the strong offer a helping hand. YOU are the master of your own destiny. Take the first steps, be strong and believe. Believe that you can and you will. Believe in the one person that will try everything to never let you down: believe in YOU. I know I do.

CHAPTER 4

All Things Meditation

What is meditation?

Meditation is a means of transforming the mind. Most meditation practices are techniques that encourage and develop concentration, clarity, emotional positivity, and give a calm view of the true nature of things. By engaging with a particular meditation practice, you learn the patterns and habits of your mind, and the practice offers methods to cultivate new, more positive ways of being. With regular work and patience, these nourishing, focused states of mind can deepen into profoundly peaceful and energised mind-sets. Such experiences can have a transformative effect and can lead to a new understanding of life.

Heavy stuff isn't it? Or is it? I have played with meditation for years: reading books, going to classes, spending a lot of money without any real results. During this time I just felt as if I was missing something, I wasn't getting it, I was lacking the key element and no matter where I went to seek the answer, I couldn't find it. In fact, the majority of the time I felt like I was being taken for a ride and meditation was a huge con. Not being one to give up, I kept at it. There had to be an answer that I was missing. Having a fascination with everything mind related, I went to see a friend of mine who is a successful hypnosis practitioner who I knew had helped a number of high profile clients achieve their goals. I went to talk about the issues I was having with meditation and ask if he was able to help me. We talked for some time and he sent me home with some breathing exercises and self-hypnosis techniques to help me relax. After practicing for a few weeks it finally clicked. BAM, it hit me. Why hadn't I been able to get it all this time? I'd been shown how someone else does it and not how I should do it myself. Classes are useful to give us a foot in the door, but meditation is a personal journey that nobody else can take for us. There is no right way, there is no wrong way, there is only our way - and if anyone tells you differently, tell them to come and see me. I'd advise everyone I know to try meditation: it's been one of the most positive experiences I have ever had the courage to challenge - and as I said earlier, I'm no expert, but I am a believer in myself and I am a believer in meditation.

As well as meditating we have mindfulness; mindfulness is a practice of waking meditation. Mindfulness gives us ability to think calmly and mindfully when life is a bitch. Mindfulness has helped me find more clarity and meaning in my life, it's taught me how to think before I react. Mindfulness has also taught me to open my mind to things that, in the past, I'd have seen as being foolish or 'mumbo-jumbo'.

There's plenty of free information on meditation online as well as taster sessions held around the country to help you find the basics, but don't get sucked in to paying for regular sessions if you're not 'feeling it'. The only person getting any rewards will be the person who says you need them, and if the truth be told, it's them that need you.

CHAPTER 5

Affirmations

Affir...what?

Affirmations really are simple. They are you, being in conscious control of your own thoughts. They are short, powerful statements. When you think them or say them, or even hear them, they become the thoughts that create your reality.

I have been using affirmations for years. We all use them day in, day out: we tell ourselves that we aren't good enough and we won't get anything from life because we aren't worth it. You know what? We don't even know that we are doing it. Affirmations actually make your subconscious thoughts conscious. Affirmations make you consciously aware of your thoughts. When you start making conscious, positive thoughts, you actually become more aware of the negative thoughts that are always threatening to take over. Being aware of your thoughts can be scary; there is a lot of stuff going on in my mind that I'd rather not delve deeper into, but that's what we need to do if we are to take back positive control of our heads. In using affirmations, I have turned my thought patterns around. Every time I think negatively, I instantly replace it with a positive thought and then another and another and another. I'm not telling you to start getting excited and run around looking for positive things to think about, not at all. I'm saying that we all have positive memories when everything was going well and life seemed to be treating us kindly. There are songs that lift our spirit, that make us want to get up and dance. There are people who make us smile whenever we meet them. There are places and experiences that excite us. We have all these tools at hand - we don't need to go anywhere, it's all in the place called our subconscious and all we need to do is learn, not to reprogram it, but teach it to live in harmony with us. I know I'm starting to sound remarkably 'hippy' and 'new-age', and yes, maybe I am - if that's what it takes to make positive changes in my life then label me as that. But - and this is a big 'but' - so what? So what if I do? We go back to the worrying what others think again, and they don't matter. If it works, who cares what negative, closed-minded, jealous people think? I know I don't, because I'm happy, I'm content in who I am. I am that I am.

We can use affirmations for plenty of other exciting things to improve our lifestyles, but that's another story. At the moment I'm more concerned with helping us take back control of our happiness, and when we have that figured out, then everything else will start falling into place. We live in a mysterious and mystical universe, and we only understand a fraction of its powers; but I believe that we, as humans, hold great power within us. Power that, if harnessed, can change our fabric of reality - and I'm not joking. I'm genuinely serious when I say we have these powers within us, power that is limitless. We only need to rely on our self-confidence to begin using it.

CHAPTER 6

All You Need is Love

'All you need is love, BA BA bababaaaa,' or so the song goes, and you know what, it's bloody right. Love is all we need. Love is one of the most important emotional tools we have, and it goes hand in hand with happiness. Happiness = Love. We don't find happiness out of love; we find love out of happiness. It's a common misconception that we need love in our lives to experience happiness. Wrong again. It's happiness we need before we can experience love. I'm not saying that you can't love without happiness - of course you can, but I'm talking about true love, love with no strings, love with no expectations, love with no pretence. I used to think that I needed to love someone - or someone needed to love me - before I could be happy, but I always felt as if I was chasing my tail, running around in circles wondering why I wasn't happy. I had it wrong. How was I to expect anyone to love me, or even want to be around me, if my face was down to the ground, if I complained about everyone and everything? How was I expected to make someone else happy if I couldn't do it for myself? We don't need external happiness; it's internal happiness we need, because without internal happiness there is only fear, sadness, loneliness and pity. These are then the only things we will attract: we will only attract our own mirror image.

I love you, I love the sky, I love my children, I love life, I love everything - even wasps. I do. I do. I do. I mean every word of it. I love my first cup of tea in the morning, I love my cat, I love everyone, and that's the way it's staying. I have no room for hate, jealousy or greed. I have no room in my life for small-minded doubters, jealous, gossipy negative people. They can all stay away. I am that I am; lovingly, happily and positively are how I choose to live my life and I believe it is down to choice that we humans have the ability to make our lives incredible! Me and you, you and me: we are creators, and with happiness, love and self-belief in our abilities, and ourselves we can achieve anything we truly want to.

Write down the names of every person in your life that means anything to you. List the things in your life you love doing. List everyone and everything that makes you feel special, and keep it safe. Look at it everyday and remember: love is all you need.

CHAPTER 7

What If?

What if I try these things and they don't work? What if you try the things and they do work? 'What if?' this, 'what if?" that, 'what if?, 'what if?': head EXPLODES! We all use the phrase 'what if', but do we use it positively? The answer is probably 'no', as it usually sets up negative quotes which we don't need. It's an excuse and a way out of doing things. How often do we say 'what if I win the lottery?' 'What if I achieve success?' 'What if I become inspirational?' 'What if I change the world?' We almost never think this way, and maybe we should. Negativity can chew us up and spit us out over and over again if we let it; we do continuously, and don't forget it's us who allowed it into our lives in the first place and it's only us that can remove it. Whilst wondering whether to write this, I considered who in the hell would want to read anything I have to say. What do I know about life? What if I write it and nobody wants to read it? What then? Well for starters, I want to read it, me. I'm writing it for myself; to help me become the best I can, to remind me that I am that I am. What do any of us really know about life? I have survived over forty years so far and I'm still in one piece - I must be doing something right, so why not write about it? If only one person enjoys it, perhaps gains happiness or fulfilment in reading it, if it only makes one person sit up and understand that life is what we make it, then great, that's a bonus. I will have achieved something no matter how big or small it may be, I know that at least I can say I tried, I had a go and I didn't give up. We are so much stronger than our doubts, far more capable of facing the challenges that come our way than we think, and through our ability to think and feel, we have dominion over all creation. We make our own world: we create it with every thought that comes into our minds and the words that leave our mouths. We are the creators of our own reality, we have free will and we shouldn't be afraid of using it. There is nothing wrong with day dreaming about a better life and having goals we want to achieve. There is nothing wrong with having ambition and self-belief. What if? What if we had all these things? What if we all succeeded? What if?

CHAPTER 8

Gratitude

One of the most important things about living a happy, loving life is how we perceive gratitude. How often do we give thanks for the good things that happen to us daily? How often do we say the words 'thank you', or 'it's my pleasure'? How often do we give any kind of acknowledgement to good people and situations that come our way? The answer is: almost never. Sit and think about your day, yesterday. Try and remember all the positive things that happened and write them down. Think about how much gratitude you felt. When you have done that, try and remember all the irritable and annoying things that happened to you and write them down. The chances are, the second list will have more on it than the first one. How much effort did you put into thinking about these? I truly believe that the words and thoughts we use every day create our reality, that we ourselves are creators. If we think or act negatively, that's what the universe will create with us. If we think or act positively, the same will happen; it's not rocket science, it's not mystical, it's simple common sense. Think about it in basic terms; if I wanted to learn about hypnosis I'd read a book on hypnosis, not a book on car maintenance. If I want to learn kitting then there is no point in me reading about origami, so if we want to be positive, why do we give so much time to all the negatives? As I said earlier, I'm no expert - who is an expert on life? Nobody. We are all guessing, each and every one of us. Some of us get things right, some of us get things wrong, but we still keep going, and if I find something that works then yes, I'll share it. I'll tell you what worked for me, not what didn't. Why would I write about that? Everything I have written here is true. I have tried each method myself and I'm not here to waste anyone's time. I find gratitude from telling you what has worked in my personal experience, as I'm grateful that they have. I am grateful for the support from my family and friends, my loved ones and for my good health, I'm grateful for my job and my lovely home. I am grateful for my voice and my sense of humour - even, for just being alive. Gratitude is free! It costs nothing! Spread it out far and wide! it never runs out or lets you down. Give gratitude and I'm telling you, it will give back to you, tenfold.

CHAPTER 9

New Things

We all like sticking to what we know; we eat the same food as always, we go to the same pub as usual, we drive the same way to work, we even take the same holidays over and over again because we like to do as we have always done. It makes us feel comfortable. We, as humans, like being comfortable. It's nice, familiar, mmmmmmm comfort...

Sorry, I lost my train of thought then.

All jokes aside, it's good to have comfort in our lives, but being too comfortable can be just as destructive as fear. When we become too comfortable, we stop dreaming. We lose sight of our goals. The 'what ifs' creep in. We start worrying about nothing and we forget to be grateful. Comfortable can be deceiving. It's good to try new foods - they keep our senses alert, its good to read - it feeds the mind, it's good to go to different places - meeting new people keeps our minds active and stimulated. We need some sort of stimulus in our lives that television and video games can't provide. I'm not saying don't watch TV or play games because we all deserve some downtime and fun, but moderation is key. Being outdoors and close to nature is spiritually refreshing - it resets the clock. A nice walk in the open airs a couple of times a week can do wonders for our mood. If you have trouble sleeping, go for a short walk, rain or shine, it doesn't matter. Go for a walk! If you can't sleep what else are you going to do? Lay awake. Counting sheep? Don't be lazy, just do it, it's for your own benefit. Add some pleasant binaural beats to your iPod - they can help calm the mind and reset the brain, helping us think more clearly and sleep more comfortably. Self-improvement is down to us. If we want to change, only we can make it happen, and we CAN make it happen. If I can do it, SO CAN YOU - we are the same, after all. We can blame everything and everyone for our misfortunes and bad luck, but it's actually our reactions to situations - not the situations themselves – that are responsible for our happiness or unhappiness. We determine how amazing we become and as I have said before, we can become anything we set our mind to. I want us to all become amazing at whatever we individually desire. A comfort zone may seem like a perfect environment, but nothing ever grows there. Stepping out into the light may be frightening, but when we adjust, we get to see the beauty that's ahead of us.

CHAPTER 10

Looking and Feeling Amazing

What do we see when we look in the mirror? Do we like what we see? We should do it us. How we present ourselves can determine our own feelings about ourselves. If we are dressed scruffily day in day out, then we are allowing ourselves to feel scruffy. If we dress like a slob then we are going to feel like a slob. If we dress smartly then we are going to feel smart. If we wear a tracksuit then... hang on, for some reason tracksuit wearers are a mystical law unto themselves, so forget that one. I guess what I'm trying to say is, if we don't make any effort with how we look, then how are we supposed to improve our minds or feel good about ourselves? Now I don't want you to dig out your best suit or ball gown, that's just getting crazy, but a nice clean, ironed outfit that fits well will work perfectly. It may only be a small gesture, but it's an effective one. Even having regular baths or showers can help us feel better about ourselves. Clean away the old you and transform into the new; a butterfly coming out of its cocoon is a good way to think about it. If we feel fresh and clean, then so will our mind. If we feel sharp, then so will our mind. Our diet is also an important factor in feeling good. Do you think you are eating healthily? Are you in shape? If your answer is 'yes', then brilliant, good for you and I really mean that, I'm proud of you – you're one step ahead. If you answer 'no' like the majority of us, what can we do about it? One of the main reasons we don't eat healthily or exercise is time. We don't have the time to prepare food with our busy lifestyles - so we have to eat on the go. We haven't got time to exercise – as it's not important enough, and takes too much time and effort. Well, to be totally truthful with you all, we need to make time to eat well and do some kind of exercise - something is always better than nothing. If we really want to do something, we can make time for it. That goes for everything I have talked about here. If we can find time to go to the pub, if we can find time to watch our favourite TV shows, if we can even find time to complain, then we can find time to do something worthwhile, to do something that can make our lives more fulfilling. We are too busy with our disordered lives to take time out to try and improve ourselves, and this, to me, is totally illogical. Is it really about not finding time, or is it simply that we can't be bothered? Because it's pointless? It will never work? Self-improvement is never pointless; making ourselves happier, loving, balanced human beings is worth the effort we put in to it. Knowing we are doing something inspirational for ourselves is unbelievably satisfying and rewarding. If we want to lose weight or get fit, it must be because we want to do it for ourselves. It's about our happiness, not anyone else's; everything we do must be for our benefit, because we want to make improvements for ourselves. Exercise and diet are important; fresh fruit and vegetables, some proteins – meat and fish - and water plenty of water. Our diet can be a huge factor in our bad health and mind. Our diet is important. It's our diet that fuels our body, and a healthy body will nourish a healthy mind.

CHAPTER 11

Don't Give Up

Well, my so-called wise words are almost over, and I hope that they have made a difference or struck a chord with you. I hope that what I have found helpful can bring happiness, love, peace and balance to your life, as it has with mine. Self-confidence is something I believe should be taught in schools, along with meditation, mindfulness, and good health and wellbeing. They are all lessons we need in our education system to help the future generations grow into well-balanced adults, and I hope to see this become reality and standard practice in years to come. Don't ever give up. Don't ever give in. If it's been achieved, then you can also achieve it. Or even, if you think it's achievable, it probably is, because what we believe, we can receive. One of the main reasons we give up is because we are doing things wrong - we just don't like admitting we are wrong. It's easier to give up and say it 'wasn't for us', when really it is for us, every inch of it. We just didn't do it properly. The time we waste telling people why we couldn't do something could have been spent finding a way and finishing what we started. I believe in you, and you should too. We are atoms from head to toe - every inch of us is made from stardust, just like everything else in the ever-expanding, mystical universe. We are all one, we are gods, and we are – as I have said - creators. We are - each and every one of us - amazing beings, and like a star in the sky, we can all shine. All we have to do is believe in ourselves and the powers we hold. We all have an exciting path we can choose to travel, and it's up to us if we stay or go. It costs us nothing to go, and we gain so much by making that move, so why do we ponder so much about the journey? Life is meant to be an adventure, so pick up your pen and start writing your own masterpiece; it's our life story, our future chapters can be anything we choose them to be. We hold the secret and narrative within us to sculpt and guide it in any direction we choose. The universe is limitless and so are we.

Thank you for taking the time to read what I have to say. If anything you have read has improved your life in any way, please contact me so I can pass on what you've found helpful. If you have found something that I've missed out in this booklet, again, please contact me so we can all benefit from our positive experiences.

Id also like to thank my support Network, without them id not be sitting down writing this Guide rite now "So Blame Them". Seriously with out them id be some Quivering Wreck feeling sorry for my self in some Alley somewhere. And I truly believe this to be the case. When I needed it, they gave me time, they showed me Love and Understanding, they showed Patience and Hope, I owe these guys and girls a lot.

I may not show it or See you guys much but you mean The World To Me and there isn't a day that goes by I don't thank the universe that you are in my life you all helped me in my time of need.

My Parents, my Sisters my amazing Children Sion And Emily, my Niece's and Nephews, Moggs, Craig, Monkey, Chainey, Chris and Cath, Egg, Pat, Gaffa, Lee, Celia, Justin and Jess, Paul and Vicky, Boggis, Doz One and Two, Amanda, Tony and Chen, Adam, Aled, Dai one and Two and Three and Four, Anthony and Tracy, Paul H, Anna, Cath, Mal, Gwyn, Owain, John, Bet, Lyn, Llinos, Hywel, Ynyr, Steve O'G, Edd, Anthony and one very special person who has shown me that love was possible again, SuperSoul. Iv probably forgotten loads of people but this book would be more like War and Peace if I carried on but I still love you all never the less

Also, feel free to contact Byw Life Sculpting for any guidance and future advice on living a happy and fulfilling life.

Geraint Rhys Benney Life and Spiritual Coach

Byw Life Sculpting

www.bywlifesculpting.com

Printed in Great Britain
by Amazon